S0-BWV-554

THE VALIANT MUSE

THE VALIANT MUSE

AN ANTHOLOGY OF POEMS
BY POETS KILLED IN
THE WORLD WAR

Edited by

FREDERIC W. ZIV

Granger Index Reprint Series

BOOKS FOR LIBRARIES PRESS
FREEPORT, NEW YORK

First Published 1936
Reprinted 1971

INTERNATIONAL STANDARD BOOK NUMBER:
0-8369-6293-1

LIBRARY OF CONGRESS CATALOG CARD NUMBER:
70-167488

PRINTED IN THE UNITED STATES OF AMERICA

TO

that valiant host whose work could not be included, yet whose poetic souls rest with them in Flanders Fields

P<small>EOPLE</small> say the poetry of our day is arid. They say that our music, literature, art—cannot compare with those of our forebears.

They have forgotten the bloody years, 1914-18, when our poets were murdered on Flanders Fields.

This anthology contains poems by poets whose promising lives were sacrificed upon the altar of the World War. All were young men—all were killed before they had come to their prime.

Alan Seeger had just turned twenty-eight when he kept his rendezvous with Death. Joyce Kilmer was thirty-one; Charles Hamilton Sorley, twenty. Julian Grenfell was twenty-seven when he was struck dead at Ypres, May 26, 1915; his brother, Billy (Gerald W. Grenfell), killed two months later, was twenty-five. Rupert Brooke was twenty-eight; Robert Sterling, twenty-two; William Hodgson, twenty-three; E. Wyndham Tennant, nineteen.

What might they not have accomplished?

Create masterpieces? They created them. They created them under the pall of rancid food, vermin-infested trenches, agonizing wounds—D<small>EATH</small>. Under these hazards and nervous tensions many sang of romance, of revelry. In none is there the ranting, fate-cursing that must be the cry of weaker men. The young and strong go first. That is the mockery of war.

The men who should be creating the poetry of our day lie stark and still.

The classicists turn their heads back toward literature's "golden" age. But we who are proud of our generation see nothing to criticize, no ground for disparaging the present. We remember the bloody years, 1914-18, and the murder of our poets.

Many of these poets have received recognition. Some of the poems are favorites in more than one country. It is my hope that this anthology will acquaint more people with the works of these fallen youths and the fact that lives and money are not the only things we lose in war. The culture of a generation was lost.

FREDERIC W. ZIV

January, 1936.

CONTENTS

Contents

Contents

Contents

THE VALIANT MUSE

I Have a Rendezvous with Death

I HAVE a rendezvous with Death
At some disputed barricade,
When Spring comes back with rustling shade
And apple blossoms fill the air—
I have a rendezvous with Death
When Spring brings back blue days and fair.

It may be he shall take my hand
And lead me into his dark land
And close my eyes and quench my breath—
It may be I shall pass him still.
I have a rendezvous with Death
On some scarred slope of battered hill,
When Spring comes round again this year
And the first meadow-flowers appear.

God knows 'twere better to be deep
Pillowed in silk and scented down,
Where Love throbs out in blissful sleep
Pulse nigh to pulse, and breath to breath,
Where hushed awakenings are dear ...
But I've a rendezvous with Death
At midnight in some flaming town,
When Spring trips north again this year,
And I to my pledged word am true,
I shall not fail that rendezvous.

Champagne, 1914-15

In the glad revels, in the happy fêtes,
　　When cheeks are flushed, and glasses gilt and
　　　　pearled
With the sweet wine of France that concentrates
　　The sunshine and the beauty of the world,

Drink sometimes, you whose footsteps yet may tread
　　The undisturbed, delightful paths of Earth,
To those whose blood, in pious duty shed,
　　Hallows the soil where that same wine had birth.

Here, by devoted comrades laid away,
　　Along our lines they slumber where they fell,
Beside the crater at the Ferme d'Alger
　　And up the bloody slopes of La Pompelle,

And round the city, whose cathedral towers
　　The enemies of Beauty dared profane,
And in the mat of multicolored flowers
　　That clothe the sunny chalk-fields of Champagne.

Under the little crosses where they rise
　　The soldier rests. Now round him undismayed
The cannon thunders, and at night he lies
　　At peace beneath the eternal fusillade. . . .

That other generations might possess—
    From shame and menace free in years to come—
A richer heritage of happiness,
    He marched to that heroic martyrdom.

Esteeming less the forfeit that he paid
    Than undishonored that his flag might float
Over the towers of liberty, he made
    His breast the bulwark and his blood the moat.

Obscurely sacrificed, his nameless tomb,
    Bare of the sculptor's art, the poet's lines,
Summer shall flush with poppy-fields in bloom,
    And Autumn yellow with maturing vines.

There the grape-pickers at their harvesting
    Shall lightly tread and load their wicker trays,
Blessing his memory as they toil and sing
    In the slant sunshine of October days...

I love to think that if my blood should be
    So privileged to sink where his has sunk,
I shall not pass from Earth entirely,
    But when the banquet rings, when healths are drunk,

And faces that the joy of living fill
    Glow radiant with laughter and good cheer,
In beaming cups some spark of me shall still
    Brim toward the lips that once I held so dear.

ALAN SEEGER
Champagne, 1914-15

So shall one coveting no higher plane
   Than nature clothes in color and flesh and tone,
Even from the grave put upward to attain
   The dreams youth cherished and missed and might
      have known;

And that strong need that strove unsatisfied
   Toward earthly beauty in all forms it wore,
Not death itself shall utterly divide
   From the belovèd shapes it thirsted for.

Alas, how many an adept for whose arms
   Life held delicious offerings perished here,
How many in the prime of all that charms,
   Crowned with all gifts that conquer and endear!

Honor them not so much with tears and flowers,
   But you with whom the sweet fulfilment lies,
Where in the anguish of atrocious hours
   Turned their last thoughts and closed their dying
      eyes.

Rather when music on bright gatherings lays
   Its tender spell, and joy is uppermost,
Be mindful of the men they were, and raise
   Your glasses to them in one silent toast.

Drink to them—amorous of dear Earth as well,
   They asked no tribute lovelier than this—
And in the wine that ripened where it fell,
   Oh, frame your lips as though it were a kiss.

4

Sonnet Sequence

1. Sending

WHEN as of old the Spartan mother sent
Her best belovèd to the perilous field,
One charge she laid upon him ere he went:
"Return, my son, or with or on thy shield."
Even so we, with anguish unrevealed
By eyes o'erbright and lips to laughter lent,
Sent forth our men to battle, nor would yield
To tears by pride's fierce barriers hardly pent.

So when they fight and all the world goes red,
No memories athwart their souls shall come
That might unman them in the hour of need,
But such brave glances veiling hearts that bleed
As those old mothers turned upon their dead
On comrade's shoulders borne triumphant home.

2. Rebellion

Was it for this, dear God, that they were born,
These sons of ours, the beautiful and brave,
To fall far from us, leaving us forlorn,
Scarce knowing even if they found a grave?
It comforts not that cheerfully they gave
Their lives for England; nay, to us, outworn
With grief, it skills but that they could not save
Themselves in saving her from shame and scorn.

5

Cometh no answer from the pitiless skies
To us in darkness for our lost ones weeping;
Their place is empty; empty as our hearts,
Or as our prayers unheeded, nor departs
The instant anguish: we but hush our cries
Lest they should trouble our belovèd sleeping.

3. Peace

Surely the bitterness of death is past,
Drained to the dregs the waters of despair,
Yea, pride on our belovèd shall outlast
All poor desiring for the things that were.
The men we wedded and the sons we bare
Died valiantly and for the right stood fast:
Yet 'twas our blood that made them strong to dare,
Our hearts that in the battle-scale were cast.

Light of our eyes for all the years to be,
Fruit of our dreams, our dearest selves fulfilled,
These have we laid as gifts on Freedom's altar
With blinding tears, yet all ungrudgingly;
Henceforth our high hearts shall not fail nor falter,
Though in them gladness be forever stilled.

Anthem for Doomed Youth

WHAT passing bells for these who die as cattle?
   Only the monstrous anger of the guns.
   Only the stuttering rifle's rapid rattle
Can patter out their hasty orisons.
No mockery for them; no prayers nor bells,
Nor any voice of mourning save the choirs,—
The shrill, demented choirs of wailing shells;
And bugles calling for them from sad shires.

What candles may be held to speed them all?
   Not in the hands of boys, but in their eyes
Shall shine the holy glimmers of goodbyes.
   The pallor of girls' brows shall be their pall;
Their flowers the tenderness of patient minds,
And each slow dusk a drawing-down of blinds.

Had I a Golden Pound

HAD I a golden pound to spend,
  My love should mend and sew no more,
And I would buy her a little quern
  Easy to turn on the kitchen floor.

And for her windows curtains white,
  With birds in flight and flowers in bloom,
To face with pride the road to town,
  And mellow down her sunlit room.

And with the silver change we'd prove
  The truth of Love to life's own end,
With hearts the years could but enbolden,
  Had I a golden pound to spend.

Soliloquy

WHEN I was young I had a care
Lest I should cheat me of my share
Of that which makes it sweet to strive
For life, and dying still survive,
A name in sunshine written higher
Than lark or poet dare aspire.

But I grew weary doing well,
Besides, 'twas sweeter in that hell,
Down with the loud banditti people
Who robbed the orchards, climbed the steeple,
For jackdaws' eggs and made the cock
Crow ere 'twas daylight on the clock.
I was so very bad the neighbors
Spoke of me at their daily labours.

And now I'm drinking wine in France,
The helpless child of circumstance.
To-morrow will be loud with war,
How will I be accounted for?

It is too late now to retrieve
A fallen dream, too late to grieve
A name unmade, but not too late
To thank the gods for what is great;
A keen-edged sword, a soldier's heart,
Is greater than a poet's art.
And greater than a poet's fame
A little grave that has no name.

9

In a Café

Kiss the maid and pass her round,
Lips like hers were made for many.
Our loves are far from us to-night,
But these red lips are sweet as any.

Let no empty glass be seen
Aloof from our good table's sparkle,
At the acme of our cheer
Here are francs to keep the circle.

They are far who miss us most—
Sip and kiss—how well we love them,
Battling through the world to keep
Their hearts at peace, their God above them.

In The Mediterranean—Going To The War

LOVELY wings of gold and green
Flit about the sounds I hear,
On my window when I lean
To the shadows cool and clear.

Roaming I am listening still,
Bending, listening overlong,
In my soul a steadier will,
In my heart a newer song.

11

"*Peace, God's Own Peace*"

1

PEACE, God's own peace,
This it is I bring you
The quiet song of sleep,
Dear tired heart, I sing you.
Dream, softly dream,
Till solemn death shall find you,
With coronals of roses
Tenderly to bind you.
Peace past understanding,
Dear tired heart, I bring you;
The quiet song of evening
Softly I sing you.

2

Once again, O earth,
Cometh thy spring;
Once again thy birth,
Thy new flowering.
After winter dearth
This prayer I bring,
God be with thee, earth,
In thy travailing.

The Marriage of Earth and Spring

Now wedded Earth puts on her splendid dress
Woven of sunshine shot through quivering green;
Now courting birds, to lure their heart's choice, preen
    Fine feather'd coats
And try a thousand times their love-song's notes;
Now little spear-point fronds of flowers press
    Their busy heads
    Through garden-beds;
And once again climbs new sap up the wood,
Making the old trees young with small buds' sheen.
Now deathless souls peep 'neath memorial stones,
To prove their bodies' immortality,
Which feed Earth's wombed children with their bones.
Now God indeed perceives 'tis very good,
    As leaning forward on his throne he hears,
    Above the constant shrilling of the spheres,
    Earth giving back to him his minstrelsy.

13

To Germany

You are blind like us. Your hurt no man designed,
And no man claimed the conquest of your land.
But gropers both through fields of thought confined
We stumble and we do not understand.
You only saw your future bigly planned,
And we, the tapering paths of our own mind,
And in each other's dearest ways we stand,
And hiss and hate. And the blind fight the blind.

When it is peace, then we may view again
With new-won eyes each other's truer form
And wonder. Grown more loving-kind and warm
We'll grasp firm hands and laugh at the old pain,
When it is peace. But until peace, the storm
The darkness and the thunder and the rain.

Sonnet

When you see millions of the mouthless dead
Across your dreams in pale battalions go,
Say not soft things as other men have said,
That you'll remember. For you need not so.
Give them not praise. For, deaf, how should they know
It is not curses heaped on each gashed head?
Nor tears. Their blind eyes see not your tears flow.
Nor honour. It is easy to be dead.
Say only this, "They are dead." Then add thereto,
"Yet many a better one has died before."
Then, scanning all the o'ercrowded mass, should you
Perceive one face that you loved heretofore,
It is a spook. None wears the face you knew.
Great death has made all his for evermore.

But a Short Time to Live

OUR little hour—how swift it flies
　　When poppies flare and lilies smile;
How soon the fleeting minute dies,
　　Leaving us but a little while
To dream our dreams, to sing our song,
　　To pick the fruit, to pluck the flower,
The Gods—They do not give us long—
　　　　One little hour.

Our little hour—how short it is
　　When Love with dew eyed loveliness
Raises her lips for ours to kiss
　　And dies within our first caress.
Youth flickers out like wind-blown flame,
　　Sweets of to-day to-morrow sour,
For Time and Death, relentless, claim
　　　　Our little hour.

Our little hour—how short a time
　　To wage our wars, to fan our hates,
To take our fill of armored crime,
　　To troop our banner, storm the gates.
Blood on the sword, our eyes blood-red,
　　Blind in our puny reign of power,
Do we forget how soon is sped
　　　　Our little hour.

16

Our little hour—how soon it dies;
    How short a time to tell our beads,
To chant our feeble Litanies,
    To think sweet thoughts, to do good deeds.
The altar lights grow pale and dim,
    The bells hang silent in the tower—
So passes with the dying hymn
                Our little hour.

The God Who Waits

THE old men in the olden days,
Who thought and worked in simple ways,
Believed in God and sought His praise.

They looked to God in daily need,
He shone in simple, homely deed;
They prayed to Him to raise their seed.

He sowed on mountain side and weald,
He steered the plough across the field,
He garnered in their harvest yield.

And if He gave them barren sod,
Or smote them with His lightning rod,
They yielded humbly to their God.

They searched the record of their days
To find and mend their evil ways,
Which made the wrath of God to blaze.

And if no evil they could find,
They did not say, "Our God is blind,"
"God's will be done," they said, resigned.

So played the old their humble part,
And lived in peace of soul and heart,
Without pretence of Reason's art.

18

But we have lost their simple creed
Of simple aim and simple need,
Of simple thought and simple deed.

Their creed has crumbled as their dust,
We do not yield their God as just,
Now question holds the place of trust.

Faith blossomed like the Holy Rod,
So grew the old men's faith in God.
We cannot tread the path they trod.

We were not born to anchored creed
That measures good and evil deed—
A guide to those who guidance need.

The God the old men hearkened to
We left, and in our image drew
And fashioned out a God anew.

That iron God, who still unfed,
Sits throned with lips that dribble red
Among the sacrificial dead.

Belching their flames between the bars,
Our fires sweep out like scimitars
Across the Eden of the stars.

And souls are sold and souls are bought,
And souls in hellish tortures wrought
To feed the mighty Juggernaut.

19

The dripping wheels go roaring by
And crush and kill us where we lie
Blaspheming God with our last cry.

Man's cry to man the heaven fills;
We hear not in our marts and mills
The silent voices of the hills:

The message of the breathing clay,
Calling us through the night and day
To come away, to come away!

For though old creeds, had we the will,
We cannot, lacking faith, fulfil,
The God above all creed waits still.

For still beyond the city gate,
The fallow fields eternal wait
For us to drive our furrow straight.

Judgment

So be it, God, I take what Thou dost give,
And gladly give what Thou dost take away.
For me Thy choice is barren days and grey.
Unquestioning Thy ordered days I live,
I do not seek to sift in Reason's sieve—
Thou rangest far beyond our Reason's sway.
We are but poor, uncomprehending clay,
For Thou to mould as Thou dost well conceive.

But when my blanched days of sorrow end,
And this poor clay for funeral is drest,
Then shall my soul to Thy Gold Gate ascend,
Then shall my soul soar up and summon Thee
To tell me why. And as Thou answerest,
So shall I judge Thee, God, not Thou judge me.

21

Magpies in Picardy

THE magpies in Picardy
Are more than I can tell.
They flicker down the dusty roads
And cast a magic spell
On the men who march through Picardy,
Through Picardy to hell.

(The blackbird flies with panic,
The swallow goes like light,
The finches move like ladies,
The owl floats by at night;
But the great and flashing magpie
He flies as artists might.)

A magpie in Picardy
Told me secret things—
Of the music in white feathers,
And the sunlight that sings
And dances in deep shadows—
He told me with his wings.

(The hawk is cruel and rigid,
He watches from a height;
The rook is slow and sombre,
The robin loves to fight;
But the great and flashing magpie
He flies as lovers might.)

22

He told me that in Picardy,
An age ago or more,
While all his fathers still were eggs,
These dusty highways bore
Brown, singing soldiers marching out
Through Picardy to war.

He said that still through chaos
Works on the ancient plan,
And two things have altered not
Since first the world began—
The beauty of the wild green earth
And the bravery of man.

(For the sparrow flies unthinking
And quarrels in his flight.
The heron trails his legs behind,
The lark goes out of sight;
But the great and flashing magpie
He flies as poets might.)

23

Sportsmen in Paradise

THEY left the fury of the fight,
　　And they were very tired.
The gates of heaven were open quite,
　　Unguarded and unwired.
There was no sound of any gun,
　　The land was still and green;
Wide hills lay silent in the sun,
　　Blue valleys slept between.

They saw far-off a little wood
　　Stand up against the skie.
Knee-deep in grass a great tree stood;
　　Some lazy cows went by . . .
There were some rooks sailed overhead,
　　And once a church-bell pealed.
"God! but it's England," someone said
　　"And there's a cricket-field!"

24

E. WYNDHAM TENNANT

Home Thoughts in Laventie

GREEN gardens in Laventie!
    Soldiers only know the street
Where the mud is churned and splashed about
    By battle-wending feet;
And yet beside one stricken house there is a glimpse
of grass.
    Look for it when you pass.

Beyond the church whose pitted spire
    Seems balanced on a strand
Of swaying stone and tottering brick
    Two roofless ruins stand,
And here behind the wreckage where the back wall
should have been
    We found a garden green.

The grass was never trodden on,
    The little path of gravel
Was overgrown with celandine,
    No other folk did travel
Along its weedy surface, but the nimble-footed mouse
    Running from house to house.

So all among the vivid blades
        Of soft and tender grass
We lay, nor heard the limber wheels
        That pass and ever pass
In noisy continuity until their stony rattle
        Seems in itself a battle.

At length we rose up from this ease
        Of tranquil happy mind,
And searched the garden's little length
        A fresh pleasaunce to find;
And there, some yellow daffodils and jasmine hanging
    high
        Did rest the tired eye.

The fairest and most fragrant
        Of the many sweets we found,
Was a little bush of Daphne flower
        Upon a grassy mound,
And so thick were the blossoms set and so divine the
    scent
        That we were well content.

Hungry for spring, I bent my head,
        The perfume fanned my face,
And all my soul was dancing
        In that little lovely place,
Dancing with a measured step from wrecked and
    shattered towns
        Away . . . upon the Downs.

I saw green banks of daffodil,
  Slim poplars in the breeze,
Great tan-brown hares in gusty March
  A-courting on the leas;
And meadows with their glittering streams, and silver
  scurrying dace,
    Home—what a perfect place!

Light After Darkness

ONCE more the Night, like some great dark drop-scene
    Eclipsing horrors for a brief entr' acte,
Descends, lead-weighty. Now the space between,
Fringed with the eager eyes of men, is racked
By spark-tailed lights, curvetting far and high,
Swift smoke-flecked coursers, raking the black sky.

And as each sinks in ashes grey, one more
Rises to fall, and so through all the hours
They strive like petty empires by the score,
Each confident of its success and powers,
And, hovering at its zenith, each will show
Pale, rigid faces, lying dead, below.

There shall they lie, tainting the innocent air,
Until the dawn, deep veiled in mournful grey,
Sadly and quietly shall lay them bare,
The broken heralds of a doleful day.

Better Far to Pass Away

BETTER far to pass away
   While the limbs are strong and young,
Ere the ending of the day,
   Ere youth's lusty song be sung.
Hot blood pulsing through the veins,
   Youth's high hope a burning fire,
Young men needs must break the chains
   That hold them from their hearts' desire.

My friends the hills, the sea, the sun,
   The winds, the woods, the clouds, the trees—
How feebly, if my youth were done,
   Could I, an old man, relish these!
With laughter, then, I'll go to greet
   What Fate has still in store for me,
And welcome Death if we should meet,
   And bear him willing company.

My share of fourscore years and ten
   I'll glady yield to any man,
And take no thought of "where" or "when,"
   Contented with my shorter span.
For I have learned what love may be,
   And found a heart that understands,
And known a comrade's constancy
   And felt the grip of friendly hands.

Come when it may, the stern decree
   For me to leave the cheery throng
And quit the sturdy company
   Of brothers that I work among.
No need for me to look askance,
   Since no regret my prospect mars.
My day was happy—and perchance
   The coming night is full of stars.

To Maude

PRIM Puritan, whose every glance belies
    The words demure wherewith you seek to guard
Th' inviolate fortress of your lips,—too hard
And chilly are such withered thoughts, their guise
Too wintry grey for you whose heart denies
    With every thrill their better reasonings.
    What shall we care if that desire that springs
In summer, vanish when the summer flies!

    You, half rejoicing, half reluctant still,
Whisper surrender as you half withdraw,
Hail me as victor, smile (none ever saw
    Such laughing mockery as that smile), until
Victorious-vanquished, as the pact is sealed,
You steal my victory, conquer as you yield!

31

The Burial of Sophocles

The First Verses

GATHER great store of roses, crimson-red
　　From ancient gardens under summer skies:
New opened buds, and some that soon must shed
　　Their leaves to earth, that all expectant lies;
Some from the paths of poets' wandering,
　　Some from the places where young lovers meet,
Some from the seats of dreamers pondering,
　　And all most richly red, and honey-sweet.

For in the splendour of the afternoon,
　　When sunshine lingers on the glittering town
And glorifies the temples wondrous-hewn
　　All set about it like a deathless crown,
We will go mingle with the solemn throng,
　　With neither eyes that weep, nor hearts that bleed,
That to his grave with slow, majestic song
　　Bears down the latest of the godlike seed.

Many a singer lies on distant isle
　　Beneath the canopy of changing sky:
Around them waves innumerable smile,
　　And o'er their head the restless seabirds cry:

32

But we will lay him far from sound of seas,
　Far from the jutting crags' unhopeful gloom,
Where there blows never wind save summer breeze,
　And where the growing rose may clasp his tomb.

And thither in the splendid nights of spring,
　When stars in legions over heaven are flung,
Shall come the ancient gods, all wondering
　Why he sings not that had so richly sung:
There Heracles with peaceful foot shall press
　The springing herbage, and Hephæstus strong,
Hera and Aphrodite's loveliness,
　And the great giver of the choric song.

And thither, after weary pilgrimage,
　From unknown lands beyond the hoary wave,
Shall travellers through every coming age
　Approach to pluck a blossom from his grave:
Some in the flush of youth, or in the prime,
　Whose life is still as heapèd gold to spend,
And some who have drunk deep of grief and time,
　And who yet linger half-afraid the end.

The Interlude

It was upon a night of spring,
Even the time when first do sing
The new-returned nightingales;
Whenas all hills and woods and dales
Are resonant with melody

33

Of songs that die not, but shall be
Unto the latest hour of time
Beyond the life of word or rime—
Whenas all brooks more softly flow
Remembering lovers long ago
That stood upon their banks and vowed,
And love was with them like a cloud:
There came one out of Athens town
In a spun robe, with sandals brown,
Just when the white ship of the moon
Had first set sail, and many a rune
Was written in the argent stars;
His feet were set towards the hills
Because he knew that there the rills
Ran down like jewels, and fairy cars
Galloped, maybe, among the dells,
And airy sprites wove fitful spells
Of gossamer and cold moonshine
Which do most mistily entwine:
And ever the hills called, and a voice
Cried: "Soon, maybe, comes thy choice
Twixt mortal immortality
Such as shall never be again,
'Twixt the most passionate-pleasant pain
And all the quiet, barren joys
That old men prate about to boys."

.   .   .   .

He wandered many nights and days—
Whose morns were always crystal clear,

34

As lay the world in still amaze
Enchanted of the springing year,
And all the nights with wakeful eyes
Watched for another dawn to rise—
Till at the last the mountain tops
Received him, which like giant props
Stand, lest the all-encircling sky
Fall down, and men be crushed and die.
And so he reached a curvèd hill
Whereon the hornèd moon did seem
Her richest radiance to spill
In an inestimable stream,
Like jewels rare of countless price,
Or wizard magic turned to ice.

    ·   ·   ·   ·   ·   ·

And as he reached the topmost crest of it,
Lo! the Olympian majesties did sit
In a most high and passionless conclave:
They ate ambrosia with their deathless lips,
And ever and anon the golden wave
Flowed of the drink divine, which only strips
This mortal frame of its mortality.
And there, and there was Aphrodite, she
That is more lovely than the golden dawn
And from a ripple of the sea was born:
And there was Hera, the imperious queen,
And Dian's chastity, that hunts unseen
What time with spring the woodland boughs are green:
And there was Pan with mirth and pleasantness,

35

And Eros' self that never knew distress
Save for the love of the fair Cretan maid;
There Hermes with the wings of speed arrayed,
And awful Zeus, the king of gods and men,
And ever at his feet Apollo sang
A measure of changing harmonies that rang
From that high mountain over all the world,
And all the sails of fighting ships were furled,
And men drew breath, and there was peace again.
But him that saw, the sight like flame,
Or depths of waters overcame:
He swooned, nor heard how ceased the choir
Of strings upon Apollo's lyre,
Nor saw he how the sweet god stood
And smiled on him in kindly mood,
And stopped, and kissed him as he lay;
Then lightly rose and turned away
To join the bright immortal throng
And make for them another song.

The Last Verses

O ageless nonpareil of stars
    That shinest through a mist of cloud,
O light beyond the prison bars
    Remote, unwavering, and proud;
Fortunate star and happy light,
Ye benison the gloom of night.

All hail, unfailing eye and hand,
　　All hail, all hail, unsilenced voice,
That makest dead men understand,
　　The very dead in graves rejoice:
Whose utterance, writ in ancient books,
Shall always live, for him that looks.

Many as leaves from autumn trees
　　The years shall flutter from on high,
And with their multiple decease
　　The souls of men shall fall and die,
Yet, while the empires turn to dust,
You shall live on, because you must.

O seven times happy he that dies
　　After the splendid harvest-tide,
When strong barns shield from winter skies
　　The grain that's rightly stored inside:
There death shall scatter no more tears
Than o'er the falling of the years:

Aye, happy seven times is he
　　Who enters not the silent doors
Before his time, but tenderly
　　Death beckons unto him, because
There's rest within for weary feet
Now all the journey is complete.

"So We Lay Down the Pen"

So we lay down the pen,
So we forbear the building of the rime,
And bid our hearts be steel for times and a time
   Till ends the strife, and then,
When the New Age is verily begun,
God grant that we may do the things undone.

Trees

I THINK that I shall never see
A poem lovely as a tree.

A tree whose hungry mouth is pressed
Against the earth's sweet flowing breast;

A tree that looks at God all day,
And lifts her leafy arms to pray;

A tree that may in summer wear
A nest of robins in her hair;

Upon whose bosom snow has lain;
Who intimately loves the rain.

Poems are made by fools like me,
But only God can make a tree.

The White Ships and the Red

WITH drooping sail and pennant
    That never a wind may reach,
They float in sunless waters
    Beside a sunless beach.
Their mighty masts and funnels
    Are white as driven snow,
And with a pallid radiance
    Their ghostly bulwarks glow.

Here is a Spanish galleon
    That once with gold was gay,
Here is a Roman trireme
    Whose hues outshone the day.
But Tyrian dyes have faded
    And prows that once were bright
With rainbow stains wear only
    Death's livid, dreadful white.

White as the ice that clove her
    That unforgotten day,
Among her pallid sisters
    The grim *Titanic* lay.
And through the leagues above her
    She looked, aghast, and said:
"What is this living ship that comes
    Where every ship is dead?"

40

The ghostly vessels trembled
  From ruined stern to prow;
What was this thing of terror
  That broke their vigil now?
Down through the startled ocean
  A mighty vessel came,
Not white, as all dead ships must be,
  But red, like living flame!

The pale green waves about her
  Were strangely, swiftly dyed,
By the great scarlet stream that flowed
  From out her wounded side.
And all the decks were scarlet
  And all her shattered crew.
She sank among the white ghost ships
  And stained them through and through.

The grim Titanic *greeted* her
  "And who art thou?" she said;
"Why dost thou join our ghostly fleet
  Arrayed in living red?
We are the ships of sorrow
  Who spend the weary night,
Until the dawn of Judgment Day,
  Obscure and still and white."

"Nay," said the scarlet visitor,
  "Though I sink through the sea

A ruined thing that was a ship
   I sink not as did ye.
For ye met with your destiny
   By storm or rock or fight,
So through the lagging centuries
   Ye wear your robes of white."

"But never crashing icebergs
   Nor honest shot of foe,
Nor hidden reef has sent me
   The way that I must go.
My wound that stains the waters,
   My blood that is like flame,
Bear witness to a loathly deed,
   A deed without a name.

"I went not forth to battle,
   I carried friendly men,
The children played about my decks,
   The women sang—and then—
And then—the sun blushed scarlet
   And heaven hid its face,
The world that God created
   Became a shameful place!

"My wrong cries out for vengeance,
   The blow that sent me here
Was aimed in Hell. My dying scream
   Has reached Jehovah's ear.

42

Not all the seven oceans
   Shall wash away the stain;
Upon a brow that wears a crown
   I am the brand of Cain."

When God's great voice assembles
   The fleet on Judgment Day,
The ghosts of ruined ships will rise
   In sea and strait and bay.
Though they have lain for ages
   Beneath the changeless flood,
They shall be white as silver.
   But one—shall be like blood.

Memorial Day
"Dulce et decorum est"

THE bugle echoes shrill and sweet,
　　But not of war it sings today.
The road is rhythmic with the feet
　　Of men-at-arms who come to pray.

The roses blossom white and red
　　On tombs where weary soldiers lie;
Flags wave above the honored dead
　　And martial music cleaves the sky.

Above their wreath-strewn graves we kneel,
　　They kept the faith and fought the fight.
Through flying lead and crimson steel
　　They plunged for Freedom and the Right.

May we, their grateful children learn
　　Their strength, who lie beneath this sod,
Who went through fire and death to earn
　　At last the accolade of God.

In shining rank on rank arrayed
　　They march, the legions of the Lord;
He is their Captain unafraid,
　　The Prince of Peace . . . Who brought a sword.

To Certain Poets

Now is the rhymer's honest trade
A thing for scornful laughter made.

The merchant's sneer, the clerk's disdain
These are the burden of our pain.

Because of you did this befall,
You brought this shame upon us all.

You little poets mincing there
With women's hearts and women's hair!

How sick Dan Chaucer's ghost must be
To hear you lisp of "Poesie"!

A heavy-handed blow, I think,
Would make your veins drip scented ink.

You strut and smirk your little while
So mildly, delicately vile!

Your tiny voices mock God's wrath,
You snails that crawl along His path!

Why, what has God or man to do
With wet, amorphous things like you?

45

This thing alone you have achieved:
Because of you, it is believed

That all who earn their bread by rhyme
Are like yourselves, exuding slime.

Oh, cease to write, for very shame,
Ere all men spit upon our name!

Take up your needles, drop your pen,
And leave the poet's craft to men!

The Servant Girl and the Grocer's Boy

HER lips' remark was: "Oh, you kid!"
Her soul spoke thus (I know it did):

"O king of realms of endless joy,
My own, my golden grocer's boy,

I am a princess forced to dwell
Within a lonely kitchen cell,

While you go dashing through the land
With loveliness on every hand.

Your whistle strikes my eager ears
Like music of the choiring spheres.

The mighty earth grows faint and reels
Beneath your thundering wagon wheels.

How keenly, perilously sweet
To cling upon that swaying seat!

How happy she who by your side
May share the splendors of that ride!

Ah, if you will not take my hand
And bear me off across the land,

47

Then, traveller from Arcady,
Remain awhile and comfort me.

What other maiden can you find
So young and delicate and kind?"

Her lips' remark was: "Oh, you kid!"
Her soul spoke thus (I know it did).

Before Action

By all the glories of the day
    And the cool evening's benison,
By that last sunset touch that lay
    Upon the hills when day was done,
By beauty lavishly outpoured,
    And blessings carelessly received,
By all the days that I have lived,
    Make me a soldier, Lord.

By all of all man's hopes and fears,
    And all the wonders poets sing,
The laughter of unclouded years,
    And every sad and lovely thing;
By the romantic ages stored
    With high endeavour that was his,
By all his mad catastrophes,
    Make me a man, O Lord.

I, that on my familiar hill
    Saw with uncomprehending eyes
A hundred of Thy sunsets spill
    Their fresh and sanguine sacrifice,
Ere the sun swings his noonday sword
    Must say good-bye to all of this;—
By all delights that I shall miss,
    Help me to die, O Lord.

49

Release

A LEAPING wind from England,
   The skies without a stain,
Clean cut against the morning
   Slim poplars after rain,
The foolish noise of sparrows
   And starlings in a wood—
After the grime of battle
   We know that these are good.

Death whining down from heaven,
   Death roaring from the ground,
Death stinking in the nostril,
   Death shrill in every sound,
Doubting we charged and conquered—
   Hopeless we struck and stood;
Now when the fight is ended
   We know that it was good.

We that have seen the strongest
   Cry like a beaten child,
The sanest eyes unholy,
   The cleanest hands defiled,
We that have known the heart-blood
   Less than the lees of wine,
We that have seen men broken,
   We know man is divine.

Reverie

AT home they see on Skiddaw
   His royal purple lie,
And autumn up in Newlands
Arrayed in russet die,
Or under burning woodland
The still lake's gramarye.
And far off and grim and sable
The menace of the Gable
Lifts up his stark aloofness
Against the western sky.

At vesper-time in Durham
The level evening falls
Upon the shadowy river
That slides by ancient walls,
Where out of crannied turrets
The mellow belfry calls.
And there sleep brings forgetting
And morning no regretting,
And love is laughter-wedded
To health in happy halls.

To John[1]

O HEART-AND-SOUL and careless played
　　Our little band of brothers,
And never recked the time would come
　　To change our games for others.
It's joy for those who played with you
　　To picture now what grace
Was in your mind and single heart
　　And in your radiant face.
Your light-foot strength by flood and field
　　For England keener glowed;
To whatsoever things are fair
　　We know, through you, the road;
Nor is our grief the less thereby;
　　O swift and strong and dear, good-bye.

[1] The Hon. John Manners.

A Private

This ploughman dead in battle slept out of doors
Many a frozen night, and merrily
Answered staid drinkers, good bedmen, and all bores:
"At Mrs. Greenland's Hawthorn Bush," said he,
"I slept." None knew which bush. Above the town,
Beyond "The Drover," a hundred spot the down
In Wiltshire. And where now at last he sleeps
More sound in France—that, too, he secret keeps.

53

Adlestrop

Yes. I remember Adlestrop—
The name, because one afternoon
Of heat the express-train drew up there
Unwontedly. It was late June.

The steam hissed. Someone cleared his throat.
No one left and no one came
On the bare platform. What I saw
Was Adlestrop—only the name.

And willows, willow-herb, and grass,
And meadows sweet, and haycocks dry,
No whit less still and lonely fair
Than the high cloudlets in the sky.

And for that minute a blackbird sang
Close by, and round him, mistier
Farther and farther, all the birds
Of Oxfordshire and Gloucestershire.

Snow

In the gloom of whiteness,
In the great silence of snow,
A child was sighing
And bitterly saying: "Oh,
They have killed a white bird up there on her nest,
The down is fluttering from her breast."
And still it fell through the dusky brightness
On the child crying for the bird of the snow.

If I Should Ever By Chance

IF I should ever by chance grow rich
I'll buy Codham, Cockridden, and Childerditch,
Roses, Pyrgo, and Lapwater,
And let them all to my elder daughter.
The rent I shall ask of her will be only
Each year's first violets, white and lonely,
The first primroses and orchises—
She must find them before I do, that is.
But if she finds a blossom on furze
Without rent they shall all for ever be hers,
Codham, Cockridden, and Childerditch,
Roses, Pyrgo, and Lapwater,—
I shall give them all to my elder daughter.

56

The Penny Whistle

THE new moon hangs like an ivory bugle
   In the naked frosty blue;
And the ghylls of the forest, already blackened
   By Winter, are blackened anew.

The brooks that cut up and increase the forest,
   As if they had never known
The sun, are roaring with black hollow voices
   Betwixt rage and a moan.

But still the caravan-hut by the hollies
   Like a kingfisher gleams between;
Round the mossed old hearth of the charcoal-burners,
   First primroses ask to be seen.

The charcoal-burners are black, but their linen
   Blows white on the line;
And white the letter the girl is reading
   Under that crescent fine:

And her brother who hides apart in a thicke
   Slowly and surely playing
On a whistle an olden nursery melody,
   Says far more than I am saying.

57

A. V. RATCLIFFE

Optimism

At last there'll dawn the last of the long year,
  Of the long year that seemed to dream no end;
Whose every dawn but turned the world more drear
  And slew some hope, or led away some friend.
Or be you dark, or buffeting, or blind,
We care not, Day, but leave not death behind.

The hours that feed on war go heavy-hearted:
  Death is no fare wherewith to make hearts fain;
Oh! we are sick to find that they who started
  With glamour in their eyes come not again.
O Day, be long and heavy if you will,
But on our hopes set not a bitter heel.

For tiny hopes, like tiny flowers of Spring,
  Will come, though death and ruin hold the land;
Though storms may roar they may not break the wing
  Of the earthed lark whose song is ever bland.
Fell year unpitiful, slow days of scorn,
Your kind shall die, and sweeter days be born.

A Christmas Prayer
From the Trenches

NOT yet for us may Christmas bring
   Good-will to men, and peace;
In our dark sky no angels sing,
   Not yet the great release
   For men, when war shall cease.

So must the guns our carols make,
   Our gifts must bullets be,
For us no Christmas bells shall see
   These ruined homes shall see
   No Christmas revelry.

In hardened hearts we fain would greet
   The Babe at Christmas born,
But lo, He comes with piercèd feet,
   Wearing a crown of thorn,—
   His side a spear has torn.

For tired eyes are all too dim,
   Our hearts too full of pain,
Our ears too deaf to hear the hymn
   Which angels sing in vain,
   "The Christ is born again."

59

O Jesus, pitiful, draw near,
That even we may see
The Little Child who knew not fear;
Thus would we picture Thee
Unmarred by agony.

O'er death and pain triumphant yet
Bid Thou Thy harpers play,
That we may hear them, and forget
Sorrow and all dismay,
And welcome Thee to stay
With us on Christmas Day.

The Cross of Wood

God be with you and us who go our way
And leave you dead upon the ground you won.
For you at last the long fatigue is done,
The hard march ended; you have rest today.

You were our friends; with you we watched the dawn
Gleam through the rain of the long winter night,
With you we laboured till the morning light
Broke on the village, shell-destroyed and torn.

Not now for you the glorious return
To steep Stroud valleys, to the Severn leas
By Tewkesbury and Gloucester, or the trees
Of Cheltenham under high Cotswold stern.

For you no medals such as others wear—
A cross of bronze for those approved brave—
To you is given, above a shallow grave,
The Wooden Cross that marks you resting there.

Rest you content; more honourable far
Than all the Orders is the Cross of Wood,
The symbol of self-sacrifice that stood
Bearing the God whose brethren you are.

61

The Road to Tartary

*O Arab! much I fear thou at Mecca's shrine wilt
never be,
For the road that thou art going is the road to Tartary.*
—SADI.

I LEFT the dusty travelled road the proper people
tread—
Like solemn sheep they troop along, Tradition at their
head;
I went by meadow, stream, and wood; I wandered at
my will;
And in my wayward ears a cry of warning echoed still:
"Beware! Beware!"—an old refrain they shouted
after me—
"The road that thou art going is the road to Tartary."

I clambered over dawn-lit hills—the dew was on my
feet;
I crossed the sullen pass at night in wind and rain
and sleet;
I followed trains of errant thought through heaven and
earth and hell,
And then I seemed to hear again that unctuous fare-
well,
For there I dreamed the little fiends were pointing all
at me:
"The road that thou art going is the road to Tartary."

From all the pious wrangling sects I set my spirit free:
I own no creed but God and Love and Immortality.
Their dogmas and their disciplines are dust and smoke
  and cloud;
They cannot see my sunlit way; and still they cry
  aloud,
From church, conventicle, and street, that warning old
  to me:
"The road that thou art going is the road to Tartary."

I found a woman God had made, the blind world
  tossed aside—
It had not dreamed the greatness hid in poverty and
  pride.
I left the world to walk with her and talk with her and
  learn
The secret things of happiness—and will I now return
To that blind, prudish world that shrugs and lifts its
  brows at me:
"The road that thou art going is the road to Tartary."

Nay; we will go together, Love—we two to greet the
  sun.
There are more roads than one to heaven, perhaps
  more heavens than one.

63

Here on the lonely heights we see things hid from
those who tread
Like sheep the dusty trodden way, Tradition at their
head.
We sense the common goal of all—in Mecca we shall
be,
Though the road that we are going seem the road to
Tartary."

The Poplars

O, A lush green English meadow—it's there that I
    would lie—
A skylark singing overhead, scarce present to the eye,
And a row of wind-blown poplars against an English
    sky.

The elm is aspiration, and death is in the yew,
And beauty dwells in every tree from Lapland to
    Peru;
But there's magic in the poplars when the wind goes
    through.

When the wind goes through the poplars and blows
    them silver white,
The wonder of the universe is flashed before my
    sight:
I see immortal visions: I know a god's delight.

I catch the secret rhythm that steals along the earth,
That swells the bud, and splits the burr, and gives the
    oak its girth,
That mocks the blight and canker with its eternal birth.

It wakes in me the savour of old forgotten things,
Before "reality" had marred the child's imaginings:
I can believe in fairies—I see their shimmering
    wings.

I see with the clear vision of that untainted prime,
Before the fool's bells jangled in and Elfland ceased
    to chime,
That sin and pain and sorrow are but a pantomime—

A dance of leaves in ether, of leaves threadbare and
    sere,
From whose decaying husks at last what glory shall
    appear
When that white winter angel leads in the happier
    year.

And so I sing the poplars; and when I come to die
I will not look for jasper walls, but cast about my eye
For a row of wind-blown poplars against an English
    sky.

How Long, O Lord?

How long, O Lord, how long, before the flood
    Of crimson-welling carnage shall abate?
From sodden plains in West and East, the blood
    Of kindly men steams up in mists of hate,
Polluting Thy clean air; and nations great
    In reputation of the arts that bind
The world with hopes of heaven, sink to the state
    Of brute barbarians, whose ferocious mind
    Gloats o'er the bloody havoc of their kind,
Not knowing love or mercy. Lord, how long
    Shall Satan in high places lead the blind
To battle for the passions of the strong?
    Oh, touch Thy children's hearts, that they may
      know
    Hate their most hateful, pride their deadliest foe.

The Hospital Ship

THERE is a green-lit hospital ship,
Green, with a crimson cross,
Lazily swaying there in the bay,
Lazily bearing my friend away,
Leaving me dull-sensed loss.
Green-lit, red-lit hospital ship,
Numb is my heart, but you carelessly dip
There in the drift of the bay.

There is a green-lit hospital ship,
Dim as the distance grows,
Speedily steaming out of the bay,
Speedily bearing my friend away
Into the orange-rose.
Green-lit, red-lit hospital ship,
Dim are my eyes, but you heedlessly slip
Out of their sight from the bay.

. . . .

There was a green-lit hospital ship,
Green, with a blood-red cross,
Lazily swaying there in the bay,
But it went out with the light of the day—
Out where the white seas toss.
Green-lit, red-lit hospital ship,
Cold are my hands and trembling my lip:
Did you make home from the bay?

68

A Prayer

LORD, if it be Thy will
That I enter the great shadowed valley that lies
Silent, just over the hill,
Grant they may say, "There's a comrade that dies
Waving his hand to us still!"

Lord, if there come the end,
Let me find space and breath all the dearest I prize
Into Thy hands to commend:
Then let me go, with my boy's laughing eyes
Smiling a word to a friend.

69

Holy Communion Service, Sulva Bay

BEHOLD a table spread!
A battered corned-beef box, a length of twine,
An altar-rail of twigs and shreds of string.
For the unseen, divine,
Uncomprehended Thing
A hallowed space amid the holy dead.

Behold a table spread!
And on a fair, white cloth the bread and wine,
The symbols of sublime compassioning,
The very outward sign
Of that the nations sing,
The body that He gave, the blood He shed.

Behold a table spread!
And kneeling soldiers in God's battle-line,
A line of homage to a mightier King:
All-knowing All-benign!
Hearing the prayers they bring,
Grant to them strength to follow where He led.

70

In Flanders Fields

In Flanders Fields the poppies blow
Between the crosses, row on row,
That mark our place; and in the sky
The larks, still bravely singing, fly
Scarce heard amid the guns below.

We are the dead. Short days ago
We lived, felt dawn, saw sunset glow,
Loved and were loved, and now we lie
In Flanders Fields.

Take up our quarrel with the foe;
To you from failing hands we throw
The torch; be yours to hold it high.
If ye break faith with us who die
We shall not sleep, though poppies grow
In Flanders Fields.

The Anxious Dead

O GUNS, fall silent till the dead men hear
Above their heads the legions pressing on;
(They fought their fight in time of bitter fear
And died not knowing how the day had gone.)

O flashing muzzles, pause, and let them see
The coming dawn that streaks the sky afar;
Then let your mighty chorus witness be
To them, the Cæsar, that we still make war.

Tell them, O guns, that we have heard their call,
That we have sworn, and will not turn aside,
That we will onward till we win or fall,
That we will keep the faith for which they died.

Bid them be patient, and some day, anon
They shall feel earth enwrapt in silence deep,
Shall greet, in wonderment, the quiet dawn,
And in content may turn them to their sleep.

The Song of an Exile

I HAVE seen the Cliffs of Dover,
  And the White Horse on the Hill;
I have walked the lanes, a rover;
  I have dreamed beside the rill;
I have known the fields' awakening
  To the gentle touch of Spring,
The joy of morning breaking,
  And the peace your twilights bring.

But I long for a sight of the pines, and the blue
  shadow under;
For the sweet-smelling gums, and the throbbing of
  African air;
For the sun and the sand, and the sound of the surf's
  ceaseless thunder,
The height, and the breadth, and the depth, and the
  nakedness there. . . .

I have listened in the gloaming
  To your poet's tales of old;
I know when I am roaming
  That I walk on hallowed mould.
I have lived and fought beside you,
  And I trow your hearts are steel;
That the nations who deride you
  Shall, like dogs, be brought to heel.

73

But I pine for the roar of the lion on the edge of the
    clearing;
The rustle of grass snake; the bird's flashing wing in
    the heath;
For the sun-shrivelled peaks of the mountains to blue
    heaven rearing;
The limitless outlook, the space, and the freedom be-
    neath.

Easter—Home Again

THE wheels of the train sing a full-toned song
As they rattle the hours of waiting along,
And soon I am swinging across the street
To the rhythm of joy that my pulses beat,
To arrive at the gate, which creaks as of old;
Its bars of iron seem like pillars of gold
Flashing behind as I leap to the top
Of the clean-scoured steps then, brought to a stop,
I ring at the bell, give the firm hand to Len,
And I'm fast in your arms and home again!

75

Last Lines

I

Ah! Hate like this would freeze our human tears,
    And stab the morning star:
Nor it, not it commands and mourns and bears
The storm and bitter glory of red war.

II

To J. H. S. M., killed in action, March 13, 1915.

O Brother, I have sung no dirge for thee:
    Nor for all time to come
Can song reveal my grief's infinity:
The menace of thy silence made me dumb.

76

Historic Oxford

Oh! Time hath loaded thee with memories
Processional. What could these piles unfold
Of war's lost travail, and the wearied cries
Of vexed warriors, struggling to hold
Their hearth secure against proud Norman arms?
—And yet the while thy quest was not forgot;
'Mid war and waste and perilous alarms
Ever thy purpose stood, and yielded not.
Noble in faith, gallant in chivalry,
Thou flung'st a radiant word to all the land,—
Pluck'd from the wealth of thy philosophy,
And to the world upon the breezes strewn;—
When, great with loyalty, thou didst withstand
The kingly perjurer in battle brave:
While England's Lady by the Winter's boon
Fled from thy peril o'er the frozen wave.
What need to tell of all thy generous sons?—
The priestly Theobald, and in his train
Master Vacarius, mighty in old law,
And the great multitudes that now remain
But shadows flitting in dim pageantry
Across the low-lit stage. In life they saw
Service of toil and striving for thy gain:
The Muse's pensioners in death they lie.
They cherish'd thee through bitter strife and strain,

77

Faithful. They fought the zealous heretic,
Rapt Wyclif, zealously to guard their Truth. . . .
Nor worthy less were they who serv'd the sick
'Mid hopeless plague, and rifled Nature's store
To bless mankind: nor who for creed or king
Chang'd learning's mantle for the arms of war,
Their lives and treasuries surrendering.
Martyrs and saints have dower'd thee: one in Truth,
Old Faith, new Hope, have died to save or mar
The idols of flown ages; for Truth's sun
Shines glad alike upon all enterprise
That in the Father's eyes
Flatters the fledgling soul till the pure heights be
    won.

These golden memories sit round thy throne—
They are all thine; and thou art all my own.

Release

THERE is a healing magic in the night,
The breeze blows cleaner than it did by day,
Forgot the fever of the fuller light,
And sorrow sinks insensibly away
As if some saint a cool white hand did lay
Upon the brow, and calm the restless brain.
The moon looks down with pale unpassioned ray—
Sufficient for the hour is its pain.
Be still and feel the night that hides away earth's
    stain.

Be still and loose the sense of God in you,
Be still and send your soul into the all,
The vasty distance where the stars shine blue,
No longer antlike on the earth to crawl.
Released from time and sense of great or
    small,
Float on the pinions of the Night-Queen's wings;
Soar till the swift inevitable fall
Will drag you back into all the world's small things;
Yet for an hour be one with all escaped things.

Rain on Your Old Tin Hat

THE mist hangs low and quiet on a ragged line of
    hills,
  There's a whispering of wind across the flat;
You'd be feeling kind of lonesome if it wasn't for one
    thing—
  The patter of the raindrops on your old tin hat.

An' you just can't help a-figuring—sitting there
    alone—
  About this war and hero stuff and that,
And you wonder if they haven't sort of got things
    twisted up,
  While the rain keeps up its patter on your old tin
    hat.

When you step off with the outfit to do your little bit,
  You're simply doing what you're s'posed to do—
And you don't take time to figure what you gain or
    what you lose,
  It's the spirit of the game that brings you through.

But back at home she's waiting, writing cheerful little
    notes,
  And every night she offers up a prayer

80

And just keeps on a-hoping that her soldier boy is
    safe—
  The mother of the boy who's over there.

And, fellows, she's the hero of this great big ugly war,
  And her prayer is on that wind across the flat;
And don't you reckon maybe it's her tears, and not
    the rain,
  That's keeping up the patter on your old tin hat?

Sonnet

Now I am free to do, and give, and pay,
   Not stinting one for other debts I owe.
   My debts were these: to smile with friendly show
On all about, too close for other play;
To say to all the nothings I could say,
   And miss the silence which my friends would know;
   To heed the clock that ticked me to and fro
To ill-done tasks, long-drawn, diluting day.

But now I am come to a wide, free space
   Of easy breath, where my straight road doth lie;
And all my debts are funded in this place
   To one debt, though the figures mount the sky.
My debts are one, my foe before my face—
   I shall not mind the paying when I die.

The Soldier's Game

HERE's a song of the game we play
    Out on the burnt maidan,
Right from Poona to Mandalay,
    "Trichy" to far Mooltan.

Sahib and Jemadar here may meet:
    Victory's laurels rest
Still with the daring, bold, and fleet
    Sons of the East or West.

Rules of precedence too we doff,
    Etiquette's self is blind;
Subalterns ride their Colonel off,
    Nor does the Colonel mind.

Here's a verse for the steeds we ride,
    Never a swerve or flinch,
Hunter's strength with a racehorse stride,
    Fourteen hands and an inch.

Arab, and Waler, and country-bred,
    Chestnut, and brown, and bay,
Sloping shoulder and lean game head,
    Built to gallop and stay.

Here's to the "one" who'll never shirk,
    Doing the thing he's told.
Here's to the "three" who knows his work
    Resolute, safe, and bold.

Here's to the "back's" unerring aim
    Never a moment late.
Here's to the man who wins the game
    Galloping hard and straight.

Blinding and dense the dust-clouds roll,
    Little the horsemen mind,
Racing hard for the distant goal,
    Thunder of hoofs behind;

On to the ball when the pace is quick,
    Galloping all the way,
Stirrup to stirrup and stick to stick—
    God, what a game to play!

This is the law that mayn't be broke,
    This is our chiefest pride;
Never a single selfish stroke,
    Every man for the side.

This is the toast we love to drink,
    Every night the same,
Bumpers all! and the glasses clink,
    "Here's to the soldier's Game!"

Life, Death and Love
An Old Song

LIFE! ah, life is a tangled webbe,
  Its threaddes ye Fates doe holde:
And as they stande, with careless hande
  Each life they interfolde:
And one by one ye dayes are donne
While ye ceaseless spynninge-wheele doth
    runne—
Till at last ye final skeine be spunne,
  And ye tale of our dayes is told,
  Ye tale of our dayes is told!

Death! ah, Death is a cruelle Kynge
  Whose hand is bare and colde:
He mute doth sitte, and ruthless slitte
  Ye threads of young and olde;
And thatte is why wyth a fearestrucke eye
Man seeth funeralles passing bye—
For he knoweth he himself muste dye
  When ye tale of hys dayes is told,
  When ye tale of hys dayes is told!

85

Love, ah, Love is a gentle queene
    And she weaveth threaddes of golde:
They somewheres shyne in every line
    With radiance sweete and bolde;
'Tis she can save the poorest slave
For she reacheth farre beyond ye grave,
And ye floore of an heavenlie path doth pave
    When ye talc of hys dayes is told,
    When ye tale of hys dayes is told!

Outward Bound

THERE'S a waterfall I'm leaving
 Running down the rocks in foam,
There's a pool for which I'm grieving
 Near the water ouzel's home,
And it's there that I'd be lying
 With the heather close at hand
And the curlews faintly crying
 'Mid the wastes of Cumberland.

While the midnight watch is winging
 Thoughts of other days arise,
I can hear the river singing
 Like the saints in Paradise;
I can see the water winking
 Like the merry eyes of Pan,
And the slow half-pounder sinking
 By the bridge's granite span.

Ah! to win them back and clamber
 Braced anew with winds I love,
From the river's stainless amber
 To the morning mist above,
See through cloud-rifts rent asunder,
 Like a painted scroll unfurled,
Ridge and hollow rolling under
 To the fringes of the world.

Now the weary guard are sleeping,
  Now the great propellers churn,
Now the harbour lights are creeping
  Into emptiness astern,
While the sentry wakes and watches
  Plunging triangles of light
Where the water leaps and catches
  At our escort in the night.

Great their happiness who seeing
  Still with unbenighted eyes
Kin of theirs who gave them being,
  Sun and earth that made them wise,
Die and feel their embers quicken
  Year by year in summer time,
When the cotton grasses thicken
  On the hills they used to climb.

Shall we also be as they be,
  Mingled with our mother clay,
Or return no more, it may be?
  Who has knowledge, who shall say?
Yet we hope that from the bosom
  Of our shaggy father Pan,
When the earth breaks into blossom
  Richer from the dust of man,

Though the high gods smite and slay us,
  Though we come not whence we go,

88

As the host of Menelaus
   Came there many years ago;
Yet the selfsame wind shall bear us
   From the same departing place
Out across the gulf of Saros
  And the peaks of Samothrace.

We shall pass in summer weather,
  We shall come at eventide,
Where the fells stand up together
   And all quiet things abide;
Mixed with cloud and wind and river,
  Sun-distilled in dew and rain.
One with Cumberland forever
  We shall not go forth again.

Sonnets

I

I SEE across the chasm of flying years
    The pyres of Dido on the vacant shore;
    I see Medea's fury and hear the roar
Of rushing flames, the new bride's burning tears;
And ever as still another vision peers
    Thro' memory's mist to stir me more and more,
    I say that surely I have lived before
And known this joy and trembled with these fears.

The passion that they show me burns so high;
    Their love, in me who have not looked on love,
So fiercely flames; so wildly comes the cry
    Of stricken women the warrior's call above,
That I would gladly lay me down and die
    To wake again where Helen and Hector move.

II

The falling rain is music overhead,
    The dark night, lit by no intruding star,
    Fit covering yields to thoughts that roam afar
And turn again familiar paths to tread,
Where many a laden hour too quickly sped
    In happier times, before the dawn of war,
    Before the spoiler had whet his sword to mar
The faithful living and the mighty dead.

It is not that my soul is weighed with woe,
But rather wonder, seeing they do but sleep.
As birds that in the sinking summer sweep
Across the heaven to happier climes to go,
So they are gone; and sometimes we must weep,
And sometimes, smiling, murmur, "Be it so!"

The New Aeneid

THESE waters saw the gilded galleys come
From the red east: the oarsmen cast their gaze
Upon its brightness, and recalled the blaze
With sorrowing hearts of once proud Ilium.
Men without homes they were, yet unafraid
Westward they fared some far-off home to seek,
Their sires, whose power revenged them on the Greek,
And round these seas a mighty empire made.
Ah, strong immortal rowers, that never were!
Leaders that lived not, deathless in the song
Sung to Rome's glory,—'mid a martial throng,
I bless the answer to an ancient prayer,
Clear-eyed to see what once was partly hid,
The splendid pageant of the Aeneid.

To An Old Lady Seen At a Guest-House for Soldiers

QUIET thou didst stand at thine appointed place,
There was no press to purchase—younger grace
Attracts the youth of valour. Thou didst not know,
Like the old, kindly Martha, to and fro
To haste. Yet one could say, "In thine I prize
The strength of calm that held in Mary's eyes."
And when they came, thy gracious smile so wrought
They knew what they were given, not that they bought.
Thou didst not tempt to vauntings, and pretence
Was dumb before thy perfect woman's sense.
Blest who have seen for they shall ever see
The radiance of thy benignity.

The Casualty Clearing Station

A BOWL of daffodils,
A crimson-quilted bed,
Sheets and pillows white as snow—
White and gold and red—
And sisters moving to and fro,
With soft and silent tread.

So all my spirit fills
With pleasure infinite,
And all the feathered wings of rest
Seem flocking from the radiant west
To bear me through the night.

See, how they close me in,
They, and the sister's arms.
One eye is closed, the other lid
Is watching how my spirit slid
Toward some red-roofed farms,
And having crept beneath them slept
Secure from war's alarms.

The Dead Heroes

FLAME out, you glorious skies,
  Welcome our brave;
Kiss their exultant eyes;
  Give what they gave.

Flash, mailed seraphim,
  Your burning spears;
New days to outflame their dim
  Heroic years.

Thrills their baptismal tread
  The bright proud air;
The embattled plumes outspread
  Burn upwards there.

Flame out, flame out, O Song!
  Star, ring to star!
Strong as our hurt is strong,
  Our children are.

Their blood is England's heart;
  By their dead hands,
It is their noble part
  That England stands.

England—Time gave them thee;
  They gave back this
To win eternity
  And claim God's kiss.

95

Marching

My eyes catch ruddy necks
Sturdily pressed back.
All a red-brick moving glint,
Like flaming pendulums, hands
Swing across the khaki—
Mustard color khaki—
To the automatic feet.

We husband the ancient glory
In these bared necks and hands.
Not broke is the forge of Mars;
But a subtler brain beats iron
To shoe the hoofs of death.
Who paws dynamic air now?—
Blind fingers loose an iron cloud
To rain immortal darkness
On strong eyes.

96

Afterward

In the afterward, when I am dead,
I want no flowers over my head.

But if Fate and the Gods are kind to me
They'll send me a Sikh half company
To fire three volleys over my head—
To sweeten my sleep, when I am dead.

And many shall sneer: But Some One shall sigh,
Yet I shall not hear them as there I lie,
For this is the law of Lover and Friend—
That all joy must finish, all feeling end.

And many shall laugh: But Some One shall weep,
Yet I shall not know—I shall lie asleep;
A worn-out body, a dried-up crust;
Ashes to ashes and dust to dust!

And they'll drink a toast up there in the Mess,
"Here's to a friend in his loneliness!"
And music and talk for a while shall cease
While my Brothers drink to their Brother's Peace.

And the Sikhs shall say (who were once mine own):
"Who rode with us often now rides alone!"
And leaning over the grave they'll sigh—
"Sahib murgya! Ki jae, Ki jae!"

97

And I, who so loved them one and all,
Shall stir no more at the bugle-call,
But another Sahib shall ride instead
At the head of my Sikhs, when I am dead.
And even this thought which hurts me so
Shall cease to trouble me when I go.

My chestnut charger, Mam'selle
(She was fleet of foot and I loved her well!)
Shall nibble the grass above my head,
Unknowing that one she loved is dead.

Some one—my Horse and my Company
Shall fail to smile at the comedy;
Shall strive to reason, yet fail to guess
That Life is little and Death is less!

And they shall sorrow a little space
Till somebody comes to fill my place;
But all their sorrow, their grief and pain,
They shall expend upon me—in vain!

And you—if you read this epitaph—
Harden your heart, I pray you, laugh!
But if you would deal with me tenderly
Place one dew-kissed violet over me;
I claim not this, and ask no more,
Yet—this was the flower that Some One wore
In the long dead days that have gone before.

98

The Wind On The Heath

THE wind blows cold today, my lass,
   And a few small drops of rain;
Then take your cloak around you, lass,
   We're off on the road again.

We two have tramped for many a mile,
   Through wintry rain and weather;
But if there's a road to be traveled yet,
   We'll travel it together.

We've rested by the hard roadside,
   Two hearts with one desire;
And Love and the Road are enough for both,
   By the side of our own camp fire.

The Gate

Musing alone beside my midnight fire
On some old tale of bygone chivalry,
I heard upon the wind's unending sigh
The muffled feet of many thousand years.
I saw them pass, gray-cloaked, and travel-stained,
Toward a crystal gate beyond the stars.
He that is called the Builder came to me
And took me by the hand, and then he spake:
"This is the Gate through which the years must pass
To be absolved from the Eternal Curse
And lay aside their shabby cloak of sin.
Brave men have brought their strength and gentleness,
Children have brought their laughter, women tears
For stones to build the Crystal Gate—and thou?

The Dream Path

WALKING my dream-paved road on the Hill of Desire
  I saw beneath me the City of Quiet Delight;
The warming rays from each home-welcoming fire
    Wove a pattern of gold on the velvet curtain of
      night.
The scent from the hill's rank grass put desire in my
      soul
    To attain to the City below in the Valley of Hope,
But my gray path led beyond the horizon's roll,
    Binding my feet in the web of a dream-made rope.
Reluctant, I followed the path, where I knew was
      Pain,
    The distance glared with a furnace glow in the sky,
And the voice of the sea and the splashing of tropic
      rain
    Were the hiss of the steam from untaught Ma-
      chinery.
My dream-path led through the Furnace, and Pain,
      and Fire—
    I could not stay nor turn from the road in flight—
But I knew it would lead me back past the Hill of
      Desire
    To the warm hearth-stones in the City of Quiet De-
      light.

101

The Hills

MUSSOORIE and Chakrata Hill
    The Jumna flows between;
And from Chakrata's hills afar
    Mussoorie's vale is seen.
The mountains sing together
In cloud or sunny weather
The Jumna, through their tether,
    Foams white, or plunges green.

The mountains stand and laugh at Time;
    They pillar up the earth,
They watch the ages pass, they bring
    New centuries to birth.
They feel the daybreak shiver,
They see Time passing ever
As flows the Jumna River,
    As breaks the white sea-surf.

They drink the sun in a golden cup,
    And in blue mist the rain;
With a sudden brightening they meet the lightning
    Or ere it strikes the plain.
They seize the sullen thunder,
And take it up for plunder,
And cast it down and under,
    And up and back again.

102

They are as changeless as the rock,
    As changeful as the sea;
They rest, but as a lover rests
    After love's ecstasy.
They watch, as a true lover
Watches the quick lights hover
About the lids that cover
    His eyes so wearily.

Heaven lies upon their breasts at night,
    Heaven kisses them at dawn;
Heaven clasps and kisses them at even
    With fire of the sun's death born.
They turn to his desire
Their bosom, flushing higher
With soft receptive fire,
    And blushing, passion-torn.

Here, in the hills of ages
    I met thee face to face;
O mother Earth, O lover Earth,
    Look down on me with grace.
Give me thy passion burning,
And thy strong patience, turning
All wrath to power, all yearning
    To truth, thy dwelling-place.

Into Battle

THE naked earth is warm with Spring,
  And with green grass and bursting trees
Leans to the sun's gaze glorying,
  And quivers in the sunny breeze;
And life is Colour and Warmth and Light,
  And a striving evermore for these;
And he is dead who will not fight;
  And who dies fighting has increase.

The fighting man shall from the sun
  Take warmth, and life from the glowing earth;
Speed with the light-foot winds to run,
  And with the trees to newer birth;
And find, when fighting shall be done,
  Great rest, and fullness after dearth.

All the bright company of heaven
  Hold him in their high comradeship,
The Dog-Star and the Sisters Seven,
  Orion's belt and sworded hip.

The woodland trees that stand together,
  They stand to him each one a friend;
They gently speak in the windy weather;
  They guide to valley and ridges' end.

The kestrel hovering by day,
　And the little owls that call by night,
Bid him be swift and keen as they,
　As keen of ear, as swift of sight.

The blackbird sings to him. "Brother, brother,
　"If this be the last song you shall sing,
"Sing well, for you may not sing another,
　"Brother, sing."

In dreary, doubtful, waiting hours,
　Before the brazen frenzy starts,
The horses show him nobler powers;
　O patient eyes, courageous hearts!

And when the burning moment breaks,
　And all things else are out of mind,
And only Joy-of-Battle takes
　Him by the throat, and makes him blind,

Through joy and blindness he shall know
　Not caring much to know, that still
Nor lead nor steel shall reach him, so
　That it be not the Destined Will.

The thundering line of battle stands,
　And in the air Death moans and sings;
But Day shall clasp him with strong hands,
　And Night shall fold him in soft wings.

To My Daughter Betty, The Gift Of God

In wiser days, my darling rosebud, blown
To beauty proud as was your mother's prime,
In that desired, delayed, incredible time,
You'll ask why I deserted you, my own,
And the dear heart that was your baby throne,
To dice with death. And, oh! they'll give you rhyme
And reason: some will call the thing sublime,
And some decry it in a knowing tone.

So here, while the mad guns curse overhead,
And tired men sigh with mud for couch and floor,
Know that we fools, now with the foolish dead,
Died not for flag, nor King, nor Emperor,—
But for a dream, born in a herdsmen's shed,
And for the secret scripture of the poor.

The Messines Road

I

THE road that runs up to Messines
    Is double locked with gates of fire,
Barred with high ramparts, and between
    The unbridged river and the wire.

None ever goes up to Messines,
    For death lurks all about the town,
Death holds the town as his demesne,
    And only Death moves up and down.

II

Choked with wild weeds, and overgrown
    With rank grass, all torn and rent
By war's opposing engines, strewn
    With debris from each day's event!

And in the dark the broken trees,
    Whose arching bows were once its shade,
Grim and distorted, ghostly ease
    In groans their souls vexed and afraid.

Yet here the farmer drove his cart,
    Here friendly folk would meet and pass,
Here bore the good wife eggs to mart
    And old and young walked up to Mass.

107

Here schoolboys lingered in the way,
  Here the bent packman laboured by,
And lovers at the end o' the day
  Whispered their secret blushingly.

A goodly road for simple needs,
  An avenue to praise and paint,
Kept by fair use from wreck and weeds,
  Blessed by the shrine of its own saint.

III

The road that runs up to Messines!
  Ah, how we guard it day and night!
And how they guard it, who o'erween
  A stricken people, with their might!

But we shall go up to Messines
  Even thro' that fire-defended gate.
Over and thro' all else between
  And give the highway back its state.

On Revisiting The Somme

Silence befits me here. I am proudly dumb,
  Here where my friends are laid in their true rest,
Some in the pride of their full stature, some
  In the first days of conscious manhood's zest:

My foot falls tenderly on this rare soil,
  That is their dust. O France, were England's gage
The fruitful squiredoms of her patient toil,
  Her noble and unparalleled heritage

Of the great globe, or all her sceptres sway
  Wherever the eternal ocean runs
Ah, all were less than this great gift today,
  She gives you in the dust of her dear sons.

Here I was with them. Silence fits me here.
  I am too proud in them to praise or grieve;
Though they to me were friends and very dear,
  I must to other battles turn, and leave
These now forever in a sacred trust—
To God their spirits, and to France their dust.

109

View-Points

ALL polished brass and varnished steel,
  Rolls the long, cool Pullman train.
Soft velvet lulls to drowsiness
  And monotone of sound the brain.

Through the sheet of plated glass
  An arid slope shows bare.
High up, the scattered flocks lie down
  Or forage for a scanty fare.

Upon the lofty hill slope, cool in the boulder's shade,
Sits Manuel, pastor of the goats, and makes his noon-
  day meal,
And sees the distant dusty train
Crawl 'round his mountain foot
And, careless and content, lies back to pick his
  stringed guitar
And watch the distant foothills waver in the sun.

Wisdom

I HAD a friend, and sometimes we would talk.
  His eyes would gleam with alien light as resolution
    burned
And he would say, "I mean to seek the source of
    thought—
  Each master only quotes in turn the sage from
    which he learned."

Upon his quest, he writes from distant schools re-
    nowned,
  But now no longer speaks of wisdom or of strength
    of will.
"Ah, lad," he asks, "what has become of my old horse
    and gun,
  And does the mist still hang above the woods on
    Hickory Hill?"

Rugby Football

(Written on Receiving the Football Match List from
Ilkley Grammar School)

You came by last night's mail
  To my strange little mud-built house,
At a time when the blues were on my trail
  And I'd little to do but grouse.
For the world seemed a-swim with ooze,
  With everything going wrong,
And though I knew that we couldn't lose,
  Yet the end of it all seemed long.
The sandbag bed felt hard,
  And exceedingly cold the rain,
But you sang to me, little green card,
  And gave me courage again;
For at sight of the old green back
  And the dear familiar crest,
I was off and away on memory's track,
Where Rumbold's Moor stands bleak and black
  And the plaintive curlews nest.
Then, thin and clear, I seemed to hear—
  Now low and sweet, now high and strong—
A note of cheer to banish fear;
  The little card sang thus his song.

112

The Song

There's a broad green field in a broad green vale,
　There's a bounding ball and a straining pack;
There's a clean cold wind blowing half a gale,
　There's a strong defence and a swift attack.
There's a roar from the "touch" like an angry sea,
　As the struggle wavers from goal to goal;
But the fight is clean as a fight should be,
　And they're friends when the ball has ceased to roll.
Clean and keen is the grand old rule,
　And heart and courage must never fail.
They are making men where the grey stone school
　Looks out on the broad green vale.
　　　Can you hear the call? Can you hear the call?
　　　Now, School! Now, School! Play up!
There's many a knock and many a fall
For those who follow a Rugger ball;
But hark!—can you hear it? Over all—
　Now, School! Now, School! Play up!

She makes her men and she sends them forth,
　O proud old mother of many sons!
The Ilkley breed has proved its worth
　Wherever the bond of Empire runs;
But near or far the summons clear
　Has sought them out from town and heath,
They've met the foeman with a cheer,
　And face to face have smiled on death.

113

They are fighting still to the grand old rule,
  That heart and courage must never fail—
If they fall, there are more where the grey stone school
  Looks out on the broad green vale.
    Can you hear the call? Can you hear the call
    That drowns the roar of Krupp?
There are many who fight and many who fall
Where the big guns play at the Kaiser's ball,
But hark!—can you hear it? Over all—
    Now, School! Now, School! Play up!

So when old age has won the fight
  That godlike youth can never win,
The mind turns from the coming night,
  To boyish visions flooding in;
And by the hearth the old man dreams
  Of school and all it meant to him,
Till in the firelight's kindly beams
  The wise old eyes grow very dim.
But he's lived his life to the grand old rule
  'That heart and courage must never fail;
So he lifts his glass to the grey stone school
  That looks on the broad green vale.
    Can you hear the call? Can you hear the call?
    Here's a toast, now! Fill the cup!
Though the shadow of fate is on the wall,
Here's a final toast ere the darkness fall—
"The days of our boyhood—best of all!"
    Now, School! Now, School! Play up!
114

Sailor, What Of The Debt We Owe You?

SAILOR, what of the debt we owe you?
　　Day or night is the peril more?
Who so dull that he fails to know you,
　　Sleepless guard of our island shore?

Safe the corn to the farmyard taken;
　　Grain ships safe upon all the seas;
Homes in peace and a faith unshaken—
　　Sailor, what do we owe for these?

Safe the clerk at his desk; the trader
　　Counts unruined his honest gain;
Safe though yonder the curst invader
　　Pours red death over hill and plain.

Sailor, what of the debt we owe you?
　　Now is the hour at last to pay,
Now in the stricken field to show you
　　What is the spirit you guard today.

115

Plymouth Sound

OBEDIENT to the echoed harbour gun
　The homing traffic on the water's breast
　Fold up their tawny wings and take their rest.
The pale-eyed stars already one by one
Steal softly forth to look upon the sun,
　So proudly parting. While from island nest,
　Deep-shadowed cove, torn slope, or purple crest,
All things give praise to God in unison.

Then, brothers—for the time is very near
　When I, the youngest floweret of the heath,
Will open in the gloomy courts of Fear,
　Perchance to crown the pallid brow of Death—
Oh, let me, clinging to the greensward here,
　Drink in God's quietness with every breath.

116

Love of Life

REACH out thy hands, thy spirit's hands, to me
   And pluck the youth, the magic from my heart—
Magic of dreams whose sensibility
Is plumed like the light; visions that start
Mad pressure in the blood; desire that thrills
The soul with mad delight: to yearning wed
All slothfulness of life; drawn from its bed
The soul of dawn across the twilight hills.
Reach out thy hands, O spirit, till I feel
That I am fully thine; for I shall live
In the proud consciousness that thou dost give,
And if thy twilight fingers round me steal
And draw me unto death—thy votary
Am I, O Life; reach out thy hands to me!

117

Cha Till Maccruimein

Departure of the 4th Camerons

THE pipes in the streets were playing bravely,
　The marching lads went by,
With merry hearts and voices singing
　My friends marched out to die;
But I was hearing a lonely pibroch
　Out of an older war,
"Farewell, farewell, farewell, MacCrimmon,
MacCrimmon comes no more."

And every lad in his heart was dreaming
　Of honour and wealth to come,
And honour and noble pride were calling
　To the tune of the pipes and drum;
But I was hearing a woman singing
　On dark Dunvegan shore,
"In battle or peace, with wealth or honour,
MacCrimmon comes no more."

And there in front of the men were marching,
　With feet that made no mark,
The grey old ghosts of the ancient fighters
　Come back again from the dark;
And in front of them all MacCrimmon piping
　A weary tune and sore,
"On the gathering day, for ever and ever,
MacCrimmon comes no more."

118

From Home

THE pale sun woke in the eastern sky
And a veil of mist was drawn
Over the faces of death and fame
When you went up in the dawn.
With never a thought of fame or death,
Only the work to do,
When you went over the top, my friends,
And I not there with you.

The veil is rent with a rifle flash
And shows me, plain to see,
Battle and bodies of men that lived
And fought along with me.
O God! it would not have been so hard
If I'd been in it too.
But you are lying stiff, my friends,
And I not there with you.

So here I sit in a pleasant room
By a comfortable fire,
With everything that a man could want,
But not the heart's desire.
So I sit thinking and dreaming still,
A dream that won't come true,
Of you in the German trench, my friends,
And I not there with you.

119

E. A. MACKINTOSH

In No Man's Land

THE hedge on the left and the trench on the right
　　And the whispering, rustling wood between,
And who knows where in the wood tonight
　　Death or capture may lurk unseen?
The open field and the figures lying
　　Under the shade of the apple-trees—
Is it the wind in the bushes sighing,
　　Or a German trying to stop a sneeze?

Louder the voices of night come thronging,
　　But over them all the sound rings clear,
Taking me back to the place of my longing
　　And the cultured sneezes I used to hear,
Lecture-time and my tutor's "hanker"
　　Stopping his period's rounded close,
Like the frozen hand of a German ranker
　　Down in a ditch with a cold in his nose.

I'm cold too, and a stealthy snuffle
　　From the man with a pistol covering me,
And the Bosche moving off with a snap and a shuffle
　　Break the windows of memory.
I can't make sure till the moon gets brighter—
　　Anyway, shooting is overbold—
Oh, damn you, get back to your trench, you blighter,
　　I really can't shoot a man with a cold.

120

1914

1. Peace

Now, God be thanked Who has matched us with His
    hour,
    And caught our youth, and wakened us from sleep-
      ing,
With hand made sure, clear eye, and sharpened power,
    To turn, like swimmers into cleanness leaping,
Glad from a world grown old and cold and weary,
    Leave the sick hearts that honour could not move,
And half-men, and their dirty songs and dreary,
    And all the little emptiness of love!

Oh! we, who have known shame, we have found re-
    lease there,
    Where there's no ill, no grief, but sleep has mend-
      ing,
    Naught broken save this body, lost but breath;
Nothing to shake the laughing heart's long peace there
    But only agony, and that has ending;
    And the worst friend and enemy is but Death.

II. *Safety*

DEAR! of all happy in the hour, most blest
    He who has found our hid security,
Assured in the dark tides of the world that rest,
    And heard our word, 'Who is so safe as we?'
We have found safety with all things undying,
    The winds, and morning, tears of men and mirth,
The deep night, and birds singing, and clouds flying,
    And sleep, and freedom, and the autumnal earth.
We have gained a peace unshaken by pain for ever.
War knows no power. Safe shall be my going,
    Secretly armed against all death's endeavour;
Safe though all safety's lost; safe where men fall;
And if these poor limbs die, safest of all.

III. *Gifts of the Dead*

BLOW out, you bugles, over the rich dead!
   There's none of these so lonely and poor of old,
   But, dying, has made us rarer gifts than gold.
These laid the world away; poured out the red
Sweet wine of youth; gave up the years to be
   Of work and joy, and that unhoped serene,
   That men call age; and those who would have been,
Their sons, they gave, their immortality.

Blow, bugles, blow! They brought us, for our dearth
   Holiness, lacked so long, and Love, and Pain.
Honour has come back, as a king, to earth,
   And paid his subjects with a royal wage;
And Nobleness walks in our ways again;
   And we have come into our heritage.

123

IV. The Dead

THESE hearts were woven of human joys and cares,
  Washed marvellously with sorrow, swift to mirth,
The years had given them kindness. Dawn was theirs,
  And sunset, and the colours of the earth.
These had seen movement, and heard music; known
  Slumber and waking; loved; gone proudly
    friended;
Felt the quick stir of wonder; sat alone;
  Touched flowers and furs and cheeks. All this is
    ended.

There are waters blown by changing winds to laughter
And lit by rich skies, all day. And after,
  Frost, with a gesture, stays the waves that dance
And wandering loveliness. He leaves a white
  Unbroken glory, a gathered radiance,
A width, a shining peace, under the night.

V. The Soldier

IF I should die, think only this of me:
    That there's some corner of a foreign field
That is for ever England. There shall be
    In that rich earth a richer dust concealed;
A dust whom England bore, shaped, made aware,
    Gave, once, her flowers to love, her ways to roam,
A body of England's, breathing English air,
    Washed by the rivers, blest by suns of home.

And think, this heart, all evil shed away,
    A pulse in the eternal mind, no less
        Gives somewhere back the thoughts by England
            given;
Her sights and sounds; dreams happy as her day;
    And laughter, learnt of friends; and gentleness,
        In hearts at peace, under an English heaven.

125

Battle Hymn

Lord God of battle and of pain,
  Of triumph and defeat,
Our human pride, our strength's disdain
  Judge from Thy mercy-seat;
Turn Thou our blows of bitter death
  To Thine appointed end;
Open our eyes to see beneath
  Each honest foe a friend. . . .

Father and Lord of friend and foe,
  All-seeing and all-wise,
Thy balm to dying hearts bestow,
  Thy sight to sightless eyes;
To the dear dead give life, where pain
  And death no more dismay,
Where, amid Love's long terrorless reign,
  All tears are wiped away.

126

Autumn In England

AUTUMN in England! God! How my heart cries
Aloud for thee, beloved pearl-gowned bride,
With tresses russet-hued and soft grey eyes
Which sometimes weep and sometimes try to hide
Sweet sadness in a smile of transient bliss,
Painting the West with blushing memories
Of Summer's hot and over-ardent kiss
Betokening farewell. . . .

Autumn in England, why art thou sublime,
So meekly mantled in thy Quaker grey?
No shining coquetry of tropic clime
Could e'er estrange me, nor could e'er allay
My longing for the country of my birth,
Where winds are passion-voiced, and lullabies
Of raging tempest rock the sons of Earth.
Autumn in England, mine till memory dies!

Fall In

Oh! we are a ragged, motley crew,
Each with a tale to tell
Of a life of ease—a life of toil,
A life lived out in hell.
Whate'er befall at the bugle call
We'll do our business well.

The bugle bawls a sharp "Fall In,"
The section sergeants shout;
A stampede on the markers,
And the company turns out.
And now you have us into line,
Just cast your eye within,
And read the tale of the soldiers hale
Who answered the cry "Fall In!"

That guy with the coat split up the back,
And his forage cap aslant,
Is a minister's son—and a son of a gun.
You should hear the bounder rant
When the rations aren't quite up to scratch,
Or his rifle jams his thumb.
He slips a cog, and a language fog
Spurts up and begins to hum.

The other with his mustache trimmed,
And puttees that need a shave,
Is a slum child from Toronto,
But a splendid chap is Dave.
His upper lip is his idol,
Boot dubbin is its pomade;
He's tried to sup from a mustache cup—
But he knows his work with a spade.

There's another chap down on the left
Who tacks M.A. to his name;
He'll talk of art or the price of wheat—
To him it's all the same.
His looks are insignificant,
In a battered pair of jeans,
No one would think that such a gink
Was a graduate of Queen's.

The sergeant of our section is
A most peculiar cuss;
He wears a serge sans chevrons,—
No need of them with us.
His rifle's carefully curried,
He's a voice like Kingdom Come;
He was a clod who carried a hod,
But can talk a drill book dumb.

The corporal with the greasy clothes,
And an eye of ebony black

129

(He got it in an argument
With the thief who stole his pack);
His office-pallored face is now
Red dyed with honest tan;
A lawyer he that was to be
A city's coming man.

Down in the motor transport lines
You will find a goggled runt
Who drives an ammunition van
Thro' mud lakes at the front.
He always has a life-sized grouch;
He grumbles at his fare;
His van floor ain't a feather bed—
And he's a millionaire.

That fellow in the ulster,
Which has seen most cruel use,
And a pair of squelching rubber boots
Which leak without excuse,
He used to be a Civil clerk,
Perched high upon a stool,
But dropped his tome to learn to comb
An ammunition mule.

Yon bulldog face with the deep-cleft chin
Is owned by a miner old,
Who has roasted in California
And frozen in Klondike cold.

His thirst is a thing to conjure with;
He shoots like the bolt of Fate;
The dug-out roars with his husky snores
When he's back from patrolling late.

Oh! we are a jolly, motley crew,
With many a tale to tell
Of a life of love, a life of hate,
A life lived out in hell.
Whate'er we've been, wipe out the sin—
We'll do our business well.

To the Dead

SINCE in the days that may not come again
The sun has shone for us on English fields,
Since we have marked the years with thanksgiving,
Nor been ungrateful for the loveliness
Which is our England, then tho' we walk no more
The woods together, lie in the grass no more,
For us the long grass blows, the woods are green,
For us the valleys smile, the streams are bright,
For us the kind sun still is comfortable
And the birds sing; and since your feet and mine
Have trod the lanes together, climbed the hills,
Then in the lanes and on the little hills
Our feet are beautiful for evermore.
And you—O if I call you, you will come
Most loved, most lovely faces of my friends
Who are so safely housed within my heart,
So parcel of this blessed spirit land
Which in my own heart is England, so possest
Of all its ways to walk familiarly
And be at home, that I can count on you,
Loving you so, being loved, to wait for me,
So may I turn me in and by some sweet
Remembered pathway find you once again.
Then we can walk together, I with you,
Or you, or you, along some quiet road,

And talk the foolish, old, forgivable talk,
And laugh together; you will turn your head,
Look as you used to look, speak as you spoke,
My friend to me, and I your friend to you.
Only when at the last, by some cross-road,
Our longer shadows, falling on the grass,
Turn us back homeward, and the setting sun
Shines like a golden glory round your head,
There will be s mething sudden and strange in you.
Then you will lean and look into my eyes,
And I shall see the bright wound at your side,
And feel the new blood flowing to my heart,
Your blood, beloved, flowing to my heart,
And I shall hear you speaking in my ear—
O not the old, forgivable, foolish talk,
But flames and exaltations, and desires,
But hopes, and comprehensions, and resolves,
But holy, incommunicable things,
That like immortal birds sing in my breast,
And springing from a fire of sacrifice,
Beat with bright wings about the throne of God.

The Eleventh Hour

Is this to live?—to cower and stand aside
While others fight and perish, day by day?
To see my loved ones slaughtered and to say—
"Bravo! bravo! how nobly you have died!"
Is this to love?—to heed my friends no more,
But watch them perish in a foreign land
Unheeded, and to give no helping hand,
But smile and say, "How terrible is War!"

Nay, this is not to love, nor this to live!
I will go forth! I hold no more aloof;
And I will give all I have to give
And leave the refuge of my father's roof:
Then, if I live, no man will say, think I,
"He lives because he did not dare to die!"

134

Belgium—1914

I.

THE lithe flames flicker through the veil of night,
  Licking with bitter tongue; and soon the dawn
Will come, and gaunt and black against the white
  Cool sky will loom a smoking home, forlorn
Of all the joy and peace that once was there.
  The pleading, pitiful dead lie mute and cold
And all untended still. The fields are bare
  Of the young green, the parent of the gold.

O little land, great-hearted, who didst give
  Thine all for sake of other's liberty,
  Knowing the cost, nor shrinking at the thought,
Be sure that thy immortal name shall live
  Writ large in thine own ashes. Men shall cry,
  "This was a nation marvellously wrought!"

II.

There came a voice from out the darkness crying—
  A pleading voice, the voice of one in thrall—
"Come, ye who pass—oh, heed ye not my sighing?
  Come and deliver! Hear, oh, hear my call!
For when the invader stood before my gate
  Demanding passage through with haughty tone,
A voice cried loud, 'Wilt thou endure this fate?
  Better have death than live when honour's flown!'

135

And so my children now lie slain by him
   I had not wronged; with strife my land is riven;
Dishonoured here I lie with fettered limb,
   To desecration all my shrines are given,
And nought remains but bondage drear and grim...
   God! Is there any justice under heaven?"

Two Julys

I WAS so vague in 1914; tossed
   Upon too many purposes, and worthless;
Moody; to this world or the other lost,
   Essential nowhere; without calm and mirthless;
And now I have gained one for many ends,
   See my straight road stretch out so white, so slender,
That happy road, the road of all my friends,
   Made glad with peace, and holy with surrender.

Proud, proud we fling to the winds of Time our token,
   And in our need there wells in us the power,
Given England's sword to keep her honour clean.
Which they shall be which pierce, and which be broken,
   We know not, but we know that every hour
We must shine brighter, take an edge more keen.

137

A Father's Advice

When I left home as a reckless boy,
  My father called me aside one day,
To give me advice and to wish me joy,
  Ere I said good-bye, and I sailed away.
And much that he said I can recall;
  And I'll write it down as a help and guide
For boys who never had father at all,
  And those who were young when their fathers died.

And here's the advice that my father gave,
  As he sat with his back to the roaring grate:
Be staunch in friendship, be loyal, be brave,
  Be as wild as you like, but you must keep straight.

Keep a stiffened lip when your luck is out,
  Stand firm to the rules which enforce the game,
Hit the biggest man when there's strife about,
  And never refer to a woman's name.

Never back a bill for your dearest friend,
  Though you feel remorse and you cause him pain;
But lend what you can if you have to lend,
  And never expect to see it again.

138

Never look for strife, he's an ugly brute,
 But meet him whenever and where he likes;
Only draw your gun when you mean to shoot,
 And strike as long as your enemy strikes.
Never force a fight on a smaller man,
 Nor turn your back on a stronger clown;
Keep standing as long as you darned well can,
 And fight like the devil when once you're down!

Choose your friends as you like, but choose them well,
 No matter whether they're rich or poor;
Never heed the stories the world will tell,
 Nor judge a man till you're really sure.
Pay respect to women and worthy age,
 Be shifted neither by wealth nor rank;
Be sage to the babe and babe to the sage,
 Ignore the man that is wrapped in swank.

You are young and reckless and overwild,
 But you live the life that you like, my son;
For in days gone by I was once a child,
 And the things you do I have also done.
Now his years are near threescore and ten,
 And he's bust his arm and he's crocked his knee;
But he holds his own in the world of men,
 And his heart is still where it used to be.

For there wasn't a man that he wouldn't fight;
 He conquered the half-cast "Kangaroo"

Who for years held London in mortal fright,
 Till he met my father in 'sixty-two.
And the man who would fight him must still be good,
 Though the frost is thick in the thatch of brown;
For I know he'd stand while he darn well could
 And fight like Hell if he once went down.

Only a Volunteer

WAR is declared in Britain, such is the news and true;
Now that the Mother's smitten, what will her litters do?
Volunteers all come forward, stand to your arms like
      men,
Let the Germans know that where'er they go,
If at home or here, they will meet their foe,
When they come to the Mother's den.

From distant farms they muster, each to the nearest
      post,
In every town they cluster, from highland towns to
      coast;
And they read the news, "You're wanted"; "Come
      into the towns and sign":
And they went not back to their farms to pack,
Or to say goodbye: but they took the track
Which would lead to the firing line.

From wives and children parted, breaking the bonds
      that bind,
Straight for the front they started, leaving their all
      behind:
And the square-heads came to Kissi, and they trekked
      on the Southern Plain;
But wherever and when they have met our men,
When they set their foot in the Mother's den,
They went back to their land again.

141

Months they have held the border, holding the foe at
    bay,
Checking the fierce marauder, giving their lives away;
Waiting for troops to help them, keeping the frontier
    clear,
And always in view when there's work to do,
Which is not such an easy "shouri" too
When you're only a Volunteer.

"Dirty, untrained and 'sidy', don't know what orders
    mean,
All of them look untidy, most of them look unclean:
Don't know how to explain it—know that there's some-
    thing queer.
Well, he's not just quite;—well, he's not quite right.
Oh, I daresay he may have the guts to fight,
But he's only a Volunteer."

Bullets, like hail, were raining, down on Longido's
    side;
The man who had had no training fell out on his face
    and died.
Dirty, untrained and clumsy, there where they fell
    they lay,
Untrained and untried, lying side by side:
They silently fought and they grimly died
In a volunt'ry sort of way.

Don't let your mind grow bitter, don't let your anger
    rise,
You are the Mother's litter, and with you her safety
    lies:
Smile at the men who mock you, laugh at the few who
    jeer,
You have held your place in your father's race,
And be proud to answer them face to face,
"I am only a Volunteer."

To My Brother

THIS will I do when we have peace again,
Peace and return, to ease my heart of pain.
Crouched in the brittle reed-beds, wrapt in gray,
I'll watch the dawning of the winter's day,
The peaceful, clinging darkness of the night
That mingles with mysterious morning light,
And graceful rushes melting in the haze;
While all around in winding waterways,
The wildfowl gabble cheerfully and low,
Or wheel with pulsing whistle to and fro,
Filling the silent dawn with joyous song,
Swelling and dying as they sweep along;
Till shadows of vague trees deceive the eyes,
And stealthily the sun begins to rise,
Striving to smear with pink the frosted sky,
And pierce the silver mist's opacity;
Until the hazy silhouettes grow clear,
And faintest hints of colouring appear,
And the slow, throbbing, red, distorted sun
Reaches the sky, and all the large mists run,
Leaving the little ones to wreathe and shiver,
Pathetic, clinging to the friendly river;
Until the watchful heron, grim and gaunt,
Shows ghostlike, standing at his chosen haunt,

And jerkily the moorhens venture out,
Spreading swift-circled ripples round about,
And softly to the ear and leisurely,
Querulous, comes the plaintive plover's cry;
And then maybe some whispering near by,
Some still small sound as of a happy sigh,
Shall steal upon my senses soft as air,
And, brother! I shall know that you are there.

And in the lazy summer nights I'll glide
Silently down the sleepy river's tide,
Listening to the music of the stream,
The plop of ponderously playful bream,
The water whispering around the boat,
And from afar the white owl's liquid note,
Lingering through the stillness soft and slow,
Watching the little yacht's red, homely glow,
Her vague reflection, and her clean-cut spars,
Ink-black against the silverness of the stars,
Stealthily slipping into nothingness;
While on the river's moon-splashed surfaces,
Tall shadows sweep. Then will I go to rest
It may be that my slumbers will be blessed
By the faint sound of your untroubled breath,
Proving your presence near, in spite of death.

145

Casualty List

How long, how long
shall there be Something
that can grind the faces of poor men
to an ultimate uniformity of dullness
and grinning trivial meanness?

Or pitchfork them at will
(cheering and singing patriotic doggerel)
to a stinking hell,
noisily, miserably;
till the inevitable comes,
and crushes them
bloodily, meanly?

146

On Going Into Action

Now the weak impulse and the blind desire
  Give way at last to the all-conquering will.
  Love now must pause, and fancy cease, until
The soul has won that freedom born of fire.
Sing, then, no songs upon the sweet voiced lyre:
  But choose some nobler instrument, whose shrill,
  Nerve-bracing notes my doubting heart shall fill
With a new courage that will never tire.
Sing me the dead men's glorious deeds again!
  Tell how they suffered, died, but would not fail!
Stir me to action! Let me feel their pain,
  Their strength, their mystery:—that at the tale
I rise with such clear purpose in my brain
  That even Hell's own gates should not prevail.

147

The Fields of the Marne

THE Fields of the Marne are growing green,
  The river murmurs on and on;
No more the hail of mitrailleuse,
  The cannon from the hills are gone.

The herder leads the sheep afield,
  Where grasses grow o'er broken blade;
And toil-worn women till the soil
  O'er human mold, in sunny glade.

The splintered shell and bayonet
  Are lost in crumbling village wall;
No sniper scans the rim of hills,
  No sentry hears the night bird call.

From blood-wet soil and sunken trench,
  The flowers bloom in summer light;
And farther down the vale beyond,
  The peasant smiles are sad, yet bright.

The wounded Marne is growing green,
  The gash of Hun no longer smarts;
Democracy is born again,
  But what about the troubled hearts?

148

Dawn At Beaumont Hamel

THE long dark night is nearly done;
   A glow-worm green gleams in the eastern sky,
The first wan struggling courier of the sun;
   And in its pallid light the star-shells die.

But now the green is shot with crimson fire,
   Which, paling, tinges all the sky with rose;
The hoar-frost shines and glints upon the wire—
   Sparkling diamonds that the Frost King sows.

The men are struggling from their dark dug-outs.
   How cold it is! They'll soon serve out the rum.
'Stand to! Turn out!' The Sergeant-Major shouts;
   And thus another weary day has come.

High Barbary

THE distant mountains' jagged, cruel line
Cuts the imagination as a blade
Of dove-grey Damascene. In many a raid
Here Barbary pirates drave the ships of wine
Back to Sicilian harbours, harried kine,
Pillaged Calabrian villages and made
The land a desolation. . . .

Saracens, Moors, Phœnicians—all the East,
Franks, Huns, Walloons, the pilgrims of the Pope,
All, all are gone. The clouds are trailing hence:
So goes to Benediction some proud priest
Sweeping the ground with embroidered golden cope.
—Go, gather up the fumes of frankincense.

Night In War Time

NIGHT and night's menace: Death hath forged a dart
Of every moment's pause and stealthy pass:
Blind terror reigns: darkly, as in a glass,
Man's wondering Soul beholds his fearful Heart,
And questions, and is shaken: and, apart,
Light Chance, the harlot-goddess, holding Mass,
Scatters her favours broadcast on the grass
As might a drunkard spill his wares in mart!

Time and sweet Order have forsaken men,
So near Eternal seems the night's foul sway:
We ask of life: "Has Chaos come again,
With Ruin, and Confusion, and Decay?"
Yet slowly, surely darkness dies: and then,
Out of the deep night's menace, dawns the Day!

151

At Last Post

Come home!—Come home!
The winds are at rest in the restful trees;
At rest are the waves of the sundown seas;
And home—they're home—
The wearied hearts and the broken lives—
At home! At ease!

To C. H. V.

WHAT shall I bring to you, wife of mine,
  When I come back from the war?
A ribbon your dear brown hair to twine?
  A shawl from a Berlin store?
Say, shall I choose you some Prussian hack
  When the Uhlans we overwhelm?
Shall I bring you a Potsdam goblet back
  And the crest from a Prince's helm?

Little you'd care what I laid at your feet,
  Ribbons or crest or shawl—
What if I bring you nothing, sweet,
  Nor maybe come home at all?
Ah, but you'll know, Brave Heart, you'll know
  Two things I'll have kept to send:
Mine honour for which you bade me go
  And my love—my love to the end.

153

ROBERT E. VERNEDE

To The United States

TRAITORS have carried the word about
   That your hearts are cold with the doubt that kills.
Fools! As though you could sink to doubt;
   You—whom the name of freedom thrills!

They fear lest we plead with you by our blood
   To throb with England in this great fight,
Caring no whit if the cause be good,
   Crying—"It's England's, account it right."

Nay, but that call would be vain indeed;
   Not thus do brothers to brothers speak.
We shall not plead with you—let them plead,
   Whose heel is set on the necks of the weak.

Let them plead who have piled the dead
   League after league in that little land,
Whose hands with the blood of babes are red,
   Red—while they'd grasp you by the hand.

Let them plead, if for shame they dare,
   Whose honour is broke and their oaths forsworn—
We shall know by the blood we share
   The answer you cannot speak for scorn.

154

To Our Fallen

YE sleepers, who will sing you?
   We can but give our tears—
Ye dead men, who shall bring you
   Fame in the coming years?
Brave souls...but who remembers
The flame that fired your embers?...
Deep, deep the sleep that holds you
   Who one time had no peers.

Yet maybe Fame's but seeming
   And praise you'd set aside,
Content to go on dreaming,
   Yea, happy to have died
If of all things you prayed for—
All things your valour paid for—
One prayer is not forgotten,
   One purchase not denied,

But God grants your dear England
   A strength that shall not cease
Till she have won for all the Earth
   From ruthless men release,
And made supreme upon her
Mercy and Truth and Honour—
Is this the thing you died for?
   Oh, Brothers, sleep in peace!

155

INDEX

157

159

160